中 ▪ 国 ▪ 历 ▪ 史 ▪ 文 ▪ 化 ▪ 名 ▪ 城

A CHINESE CITY OF HISTORICAL AND CULTURAL FAME

# 苏州

# SUZHOU

古吴轩出版社

GUWUXUAN PUBLISHING HOUSE

**主　　编**：陆祖康
**副 主 编**：徐文涛　邱晓翔
**编　　委**：陈健行　顾建中　卢彩萍　兰　兰　朱昂林　莫汝和　向福森　姜　伟
**摄　　影**：陈健行　缪立群　郑可俊　唐嘉鸿　刘智常　张炎龙　程晓中　凌　奕
钱桂锋　查正风　未　名　海　涌　文　力　金　月　杭兴微　濮建明
汝　和　家　宏　姚　力　陆卫东　赵家胜　邱云峰等
**撰　　稿**：文　力　海　涌　金　月　卢彩萍　汝　和　谈忠毅　尤德荣等
**翻　　译**：沈仲辉

**图书在版编目(CIP)数据**
苏州:汉英对照/陆祖康主编.-苏州：古吴轩出版社，2000.12
(中国历史文化名城)
ISBN 7-80574-511-0

I.苏...Ⅱ.陆... Ⅲ.名胜古迹-江苏-苏州市-摄影集-汉、英
Ⅳ.K928.705.33-64
中国版本图书馆CIP数据核字(2000)第41860号

**策　　划**：顾鉴明　　**责任编辑**：顾鉴明
**美术编辑**：唐伟明　　**封面设计**：何　洁　　**责任印刷**：蒋家宏
**出版发行**：古吴轩出版社
**地　　址**：苏州市人民路憩桥巷9号　215002
**制　　版**：苏州八方制版有限公司
**印　　制**：上海界龙装订印刷厂
**版　　次**：2000年12月第一版、第一次印刷
**印　　数**：1-8000
**开　　本**：889×1194毫米 1/48 2.5印张
**书　　号**：ISBN 7-80574-511-0/J·403
002800

# 总　　序

保护和发展城市的历史文化是当今全世界都在关心的重要问题。我国以其光辉独特的历史文化屹立于世界民族之林，历史文化名城更是中华民族的瑰宝。1982年以来，政府已陆续命名了数批重点保护的国家级历史文化名城。保护历史文化不仅仅是历史文化名城的问题，每一个城市都有自己的历史文化，一个没有自己文化和文明的城市，是算不上一个现代化城市的。所以，各个城市特别是历史文化名城都应在保护中努力发展符合本身特色的文化、经济、旅游等事业，以求继往开来，永葆青春。国家历史文化名城研究中心和古吴轩出版社组织编辑的《中国历史文化名城》系列画册，无疑将为更好地宣传、保护、发展名城起到有益的作用。

全国历史文化名城保护专家委员会主任
中国科学院院士、中国工程院院士　周干峙

## PREFACE TO THE ALBUM SERIES

It is a matter of worldwide concern to protect and promote the history and culture of the cities. China is recognized by the entire world for her brilliant history and culture, and the cities of historical and cultural fame are a treasure of the Chinese nation. Since 1982, the State has nominated several groups of cities of historical and cultural fame to be protected at the national level. The preservation of history and culture does not only concern the cities of historical and cultural fame. Every city, without exception, has its own history and culture. A city without history and culture cannot be considered a modern city. In the course of the protection, every city, especially those of historical and cultural fame, should therefore endeavor to promote its culture, economy, and tourism, etc. in the light of its own characteristics so as to blaze new trails and maintain its vitality. The series of albums, "the Chinese Cities of Historical and Cultural Fame", edited by National Research Center of Cities of Historical and Cultural Fame and Guwuxuan Publishing House, will undoubtedly play a significant part in the promotion, protection, and development of the cities of fame.

**Zhou Ganshi**

Chairman of National Experts' Committee for the Protection of Cities of Historical and Cultural Fame,

Member of China Academy of Sciences,

Member of China Academy of Engineering

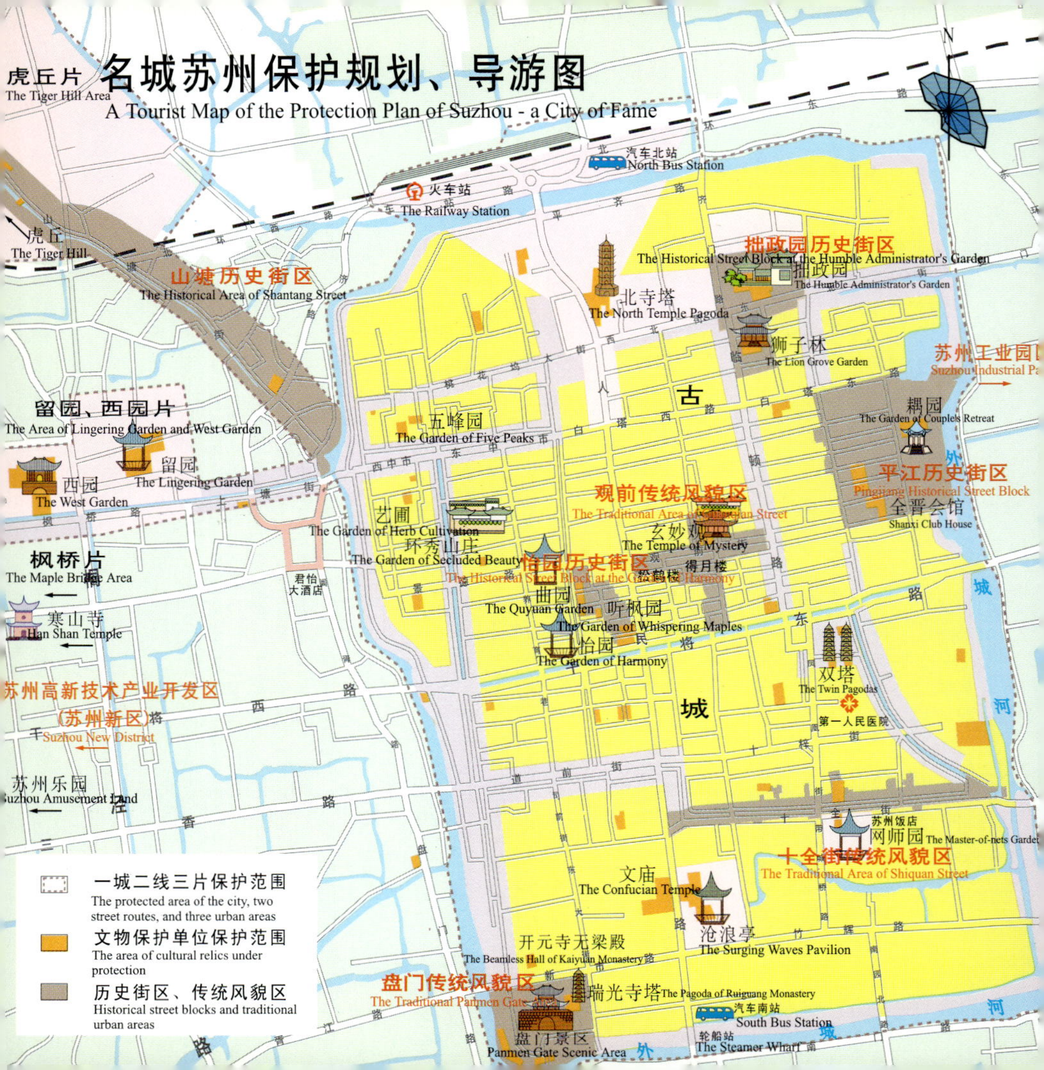

名城苏州保护规划、导游图
A Tourist Map of the Protection Plan of Suzhou - a City of Fame
虎丘片
The Tiger Hill Area
虎丘
The Tiger Hill
汽车北站
North Bus Station
火车站
The Railway Station
山塘历史街区
The Historical Area of Shantang Street
拙政园历史街区
The Historical Street Block at the Humble Administrator's Garden
拙政园
The Humble Administrator's Garden
北寺塔
The North Temple Pagoda
狮子林
The Lion Grove Garden
苏州工业园区
Suzhou Industrial Pa
留园、西园片
The Area of Lingering Garden and West Garden
留园
The Lingering Garden
西园
The West Garden
五峰园
The Garden of Five Peaks
耦园
The Garden of Couples Retreat
平江历史街区
Pingjiang Historical Street Block
全晋会馆
Shanxi Club House
观前传统风貌区
玄妙观
The Temple of Mystery
艺圃
The Garden of Herb Cultivation
环秀山庄
The Garden of Secluded Beauty
怡园历史街区
得月楼
君怡大酒店
枫桥片
The Maple Bridge Area
寒山寺
Han Shan Temple
曲园
The Quyuan Garden
听枫园
The Garden of Whispering Maples
怡园
The Garden of Harmony
双塔
The Twin Pagodas
第一人民医院
古
城
苏州高新技术产业开发区
(苏州新区)
Suzhou New District
苏州乐园
Suzhou Amusement Land
苏州饭店
网师园
The Master-of-nets Garden
十全街传统风貌区
The Traditional Area of Shiquan Street
文庙
The Confucian Temple
沧浪亭
The Surging Waves Pavilion
开元寺无梁殿
The Beamless Hall of Kaiyuan Monastery
盘门传统风貌区
瑞光寺塔
The Pagoda of Ruiguang Monastery
汽车南站
South Bus Station
轮船站
The Steamer Wharf
盘门景区
Panmen Gate Scenic Area
一城二线三片保护范围
The protected area of the city, two street routes, and three urban areas
文物保护单位保护范围
The area of cultural relics under protection
历史街区、传统风貌区
Historical street blocks and traditional urban areas

# 目　录
# CONTENTS

# 名城苏州

苏州，始称吴，又名“吴门”、“姑苏”，位于长江三角洲，面积8848.4平方公里（其中古城为14.2平方公里），人口570余万。境内河流湖泊密布，京杭大运河纵贯南北，是著名的江南水乡。

公元前514年，吴王阖闾于此建都设城。2500多年来，苏州历经沧桑，但至今城址未变，古城内仍保持着“水陆平行，河街相邻”的双棋盘格局和粉墙黛瓦、小桥流水的古朴风貌。1982年，被国务院公布为第一批国家级历史文化名城。

苏州是我国著名的风景旅游城市，享有“人间天堂”之美誉。古城西南的太湖为国家重点风景名胜区，碧波万顷，风光秀丽，13个景区中8个在苏州。其中洞庭东、西山及天平、灵岩、穹窿、天池、邓尉诸名山景色奇绝、人文景观丰富，均为著名的旅游胜地。

苏州既有山水之胜，更有园林之美。现存的60多处古典园林，集自然美和艺术美于一体，是建筑、山水、花木、雕刻、书画等诸多门类的综合艺术品。其中拙政园、留园、网师园、环秀山庄等已列入联合国《世界文化遗产名录》。

苏州古城周边的周庄、同里、角直、木渎、光福、东山等镇，仍保持着原汁原味的古镇风貌，如颗颗明珠镶嵌在太湖之滨、江南大地。其中周庄、同里、角直正在申报世界文化遗产。

苏州，是吴文化的重要发源地。苏绣、绘画、篆刻、昆曲、评弹、苏剧以及饮食、服饰、语言等融汇成其丰富内涵。孙武、陆逊、顾野王、范仲淹、文徵明、柳亚子等历代名人为苏州的历

玉璧（新石器）
*A jade ornament (Neolithic Times).*

提梁盉（春秋）
*The tripot with a handle (from Spring and Autumn Period).*

史增光添彩。

苏州素有“鱼米之乡”、“丝绸之府”、“工艺之都”之称，是江南富庶丰裕之地。改革开放以来，发展更为迅速，已成为长江三角洲重要的经济中心之一。外向型经济成为苏州经济的重要支柱，目前世界500强企业中已有77家来苏投资办厂，5个国家级和10个省级开发区建设保持良好的发展势头。

继往开来，苏州的明天更美好！

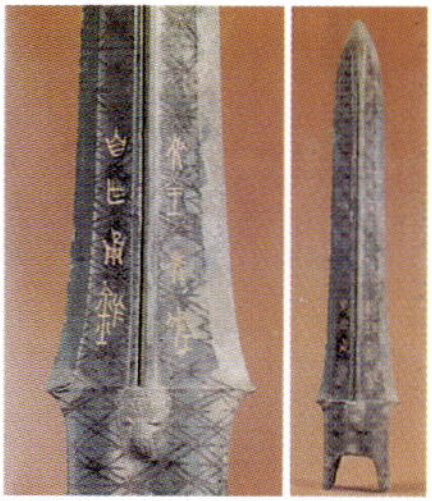

吴王夫差矛（春秋）
*The Spear of Fu Chai of Wu State (from Spring and Autumn Period).*

青瓷五连罐（三国）
*5-chain celadon jar (from Three Kingdoms Period).*

## SUZHOU, A CITY OF FAME

Suzhou, originally known as "Wu" and later as "Wumen" and "Gusu", is situated in the southern Yangtze Delta with an area of 8848.4 square kilometers (14.2 square kilometers of which belong to the old city proper), and a population of over 5.7 million. Covered with Numerous lakes and waterways, including the Beijing-Hangzhou Grand Canal passing through from north to south, the area is well known as a water country in the southern Yangtze Delta.

In 514 BC, King He Lu of Wu State built his capital here, and ever since then, the ancient city of Suzhou has remained on its original site for over 2,500 years despite the passages of time. The old city proper has retained till this day the ancient form of double-line chessboard, with streets and canals going on parallel, and the sight of white walls and dark roof-tiles, and delicate bridges over flowing waters. In 1982, Suzhou was listed by the State Council as one of the first cities of historical and cultural renown at the national level.

Reputed as "paradise on earth", Suzhou is a major Chinese city of scenic and tourist attraction. The expansive and charming Lake Tai, to the southwest of the ancient city, is a major national scenic zone, divided into 13 scenic areas, 8 of which are located within the boundaries of Suzhou, such as the tourist spots of East and West Dongting Hills, Tianping Hill, Lingyan Hill, Conglong

Mountain, Tianchi Hill, and Dengwei Hill, etc., all with natural beauty and rich historical interest.

Apart from the elegant hills and waters, Suzhou is also famous for its elegant classical gardens, which number over 60 today. They are an integrated art of architecture, landscaping, trees and flowers, carving, and calligraphy and painting, etc. Among them, the Humble Administrator's Garden, the Lingering Garden, the Master-of-Nets Garden, the Mountain Villa of Secluded Beauty, have been listed as "World Cultural Heritage".

Scattered around the ancient city of Suzhou like lustrous gems in the Lake Tai Valley are a number of ancient towns: Zhouzhuang, Tongli, Luzhi, Mudu, Guangfu, and East Hill, which have maintained the original outlook of antiquity. The Towns of Zhouzhuang, Tongli and Luzhi are currently applying for the listing of World Cultural Heritage.

Suzhou is the cradle of Wu Culture, reflected in the art of Suzhou embroidery, painting, seal engraving, Kunqu Opera, Suzhou Ballad Singing, Suzhou Opera, cuisine, costume, and the local dialect, etc. A lot of luster has been added to the history of Suzhou by such great figures as Sun Wu, Lu Xun, Gu Yewang, Fan Zhongyan, Wen Zhenming, and Liu Yazi, etc.

Known since ancient times as "land of fish and rice", "home of silk", and "metropolis of arts and crafts", Suzhou is a land of plenty in the southern Yangtze Delta. With accelerated development since the reform and opening up, Suzhou has become an important economic center in the area south of the Yangtze, where external-oriented economy has become the mainstay of Suzhou's economy. At present, 77 companies from the Fortune 500 have settled in Suzhou with invested manufacturing in the 5 national and 10 provincial economic development zones, which are showing bright prospect.

A brighter future can be anticipated for Suzhou.

**图例** *Legend*

世界文化遗产
*World Cultural Heritage*

- 已列入 *Officially Listed*
- 已申报 *Applied for Listing*

文物保护单位
*Unit of Cultural Relic*

- ●●● 国家级 *At the National Level*
- ●● 省级 *At the Provincial Level*
- ● 市（县）级 *At the Municipal (or County) Level*

越窑青瓷莲花碗 （五代）
*Lotus-shaped celadon bowl from the Yue Kiln.*

**平江图** ●●●

宋代苏州称“平江府”。平江图为我国最早、最详细准确的石刻城市平面图，刻于宋绍定二年（1229年）。右图为其局部。

*THE MAP OF PINGJIANG*

*Suzhou was called Pingjiang during the Song period, and the map of Pingjiang is the earliest and most detailed stone carved floor map of the city, carved in the 2nd year of Shao Ding Reign of the Song Dynasty (1229 AD). Photo shows the carved map.*

盘门 *Panmen Gate.*

## 盘门景区

位于古城西南隅。盘门始建于春秋吴王阖闾元年（前514年），是我国保存最完整的水陆并峙的古城门。城墙础石等可辨认出唐以后历代修筑的痕迹。盘门与建于宋代的瑞光寺塔、始建于宋代的吴门桥以及伍相祠、丽景楼等一起构成盘门景区。

### *PANMEN GATE SCENIC AREA*

*Located on the southwest of the city, Panmen Gate, built in the first year of the reign of King He Lu of Wu State (514 BC), is the earliest ancient city gate in good state of preservation in China, where land and water gates stand side by side. The foundation stones of the city wall are evidence to the repairs carried out in the different times since the Tang Dynasty. Together with Ruiguang Pagoda and Wumen Bridge of the Song period and other historical buildings like Wu Zixu's Shrine and Lijing Tower, it forms Panmen Gate scenic area.*

瑞光寺塔 *The Pagoda of Ruiguang Monastery.*

吴门桥 *Wumen Bridge.*

太平天国忠王府 *Residence of Faithful Prince.*

### 太平天国忠王府

位于东北街。1860年太平军攻克苏州后，将拙政园及附近第宅园林，逐步改建为忠王府。梁上所存太平天国彩画弥足珍贵。

### *RESIDENCE OF FAITHFUL PRINCE*

*Located on Dongbei Street, the Residence of Faithful Prince was a renovation on the site of Humble Administrator's Garden and the neighboring courtyards houses after the troops of Taipings captured Suzhou in 1860. The original colored paintings on the beams of the residence are of special value.*

### 俞樾故居

位于人民路马医科巷。清儒学宗师俞樾建于同治十三年（1874年），建筑素朴典雅，主建筑有春在堂等。

### *FORMER RESIDENCE OF YU YUE*

*Located in Mayike Lane near Renmin Road, it was built in the 13th year of Tongzhi Reign of the Qing Dynasty (1871) by Yu Yue, the great Confucian scholar, in a style of elegant simplicity. Among the major buildings is the Hall of Ever-present Spring.*

## 王鳌祠

地处景德路，明始建。王鏊，吴县东山人，官至户部尚书、文渊阁大学士。

*SHRINE OF WANG AO*

*Located on Jingde Road, it was first built during the Ming Dynasty. Wang Ao, a native from East Hill of Wuxian County, was once the Finance Minister and Imperial Academician of the Ming regime.*

俞樾故居 *Former Residence of Yu Yue.*

王鏊祠 *Shrine of Wang Ao.*

北寺塔 *The North Temple Pagoda.*

## 古 塔

苏州古塔颇多，旧有“七塔”之说。位于人民路北端的北寺塔，始建于南朝梁，宋重建，为我国现存最高大的砖木结构古塔。罗汉院双塔位于定慧寺巷，宋太平兴国七年（982年）始建。甲辰巷砖塔位于干将路甲辰巷，始建于宋，全塔均用青砖筑砌。

*ANCIENT PAGODAS*

*Pagodas abound in the city of Suzhou, popularly known for its seven pagodas. The North Temple Pagoda on the northern end of Renmin Road, first built during the Liang of Southern Dynasties and renovated in the Song, is the most imposing pagoda of wood and brick structure in China. The Twin Pagodas in the Arhat Hall in Dinghuisi Lane was first built in the 7th year of Tai Ping Xing Guo Reign of the Song Dynasty (982 AD). The Brick Pagoda, in Jachen Lane near Ganjiang Road, was first built entirely with dark grey bricks in the Song Dynasty.*

罗汉院双塔 *The Twin Pagodas in the Hall of Arhats.*

甲辰巷砖塔 *The Brick Pagoda in Jachen Lane.*

### 玄妙观三清殿

位于观前街。道观创于晋咸宁二年（276年），初名真庆道院，宋名天庆观，元始称玄妙观。屡经兴废。盛时有大小殿宇30余座。现存三清殿为宋淳熙六年（1179年）重建，规模宏大，结构富有特色。

### *THE HALL OF THREE PURITIES IN THE TEMPLE OF MYSTERY*

*Loacted on Guanqian Street, the Taoist temple was built in the 2nd year of Xianning Reign of the Jin Dynasty (276 AD) with the name of Zhenqing Taoist Temple, renamed as Tian Qing Temple in the Song, and Temple of Mystery during the Yuan. There were once as many as over 30 halls at its zenith. The existing Hall of Three Purities, a renovation from the 6th year of Chunxi Reign of the Song (1179 AD), is of a majestic structure in a unique style.*

全晋会馆 *The Shanxi Club Hall.*





## 全晋会馆

位于中张家巷。建于清光绪五年（1879年），是苏州现存最完整的会馆之一。馆内古戏台雕梁画栋，建筑精美。

*SHANXI CLUB HALL*

*First built in Zhongzhangjia Lane in the 5th year of Guangxu Reign of the Qing (1879 AD), it is the most extant club building in present-day Suzhou. The traditional stage inside the club is an exquisite architecture with elaborate carvings and paintings.*

## 开元寺无梁殿

位于东大街，即藏经阁。建于明万历四十六年（1618年），采用砖拱券取代梁架木结构，故俗称无梁殿。

*THE BEAMLESS HALL IN KAIYUAN TEMPLE*

*Located on Dongda Street, it was originally built as a storage of Buddhist scriptures in the 46th year of Wan Li Reign of the Ming (1618 AD). Brick brackets were used to replace the wooden framework, hence the name.*

开元寺无梁殿 *The Beamless Hall in Kaiyuan Temple.*

**过云楼**

位于干将西路。建于清，为藏书家顾文彬故居。

*GUOYUN TOWER*

*It was built in the Qing period on West Ganjiang Road as the residence of Gu Wenbin, a well-known collector of books.*

**东吴大学旧址**

位于十梓街。苏州大学前身，建于清光绪二十七年（1901年）。

*THE SITE OF FORMER SOOCHOW UNIVERSITY*

*On Shizi Street, it was established in the 27 year of Guangxu Reign of the Qing (1901 AD) as the origin of today's Suzhou University.*

## 古城保护

1986年，国务院批复中要求“全面保护苏州古城风貌”，即主要保护“一城（古城）二线（山塘街、河，上塘街、河与枫桥路）三片（西园、留园景区，枫桥镇，虎丘景区）”。平江水巷位于古城东北隅，前街后河，户户枕水而居，依然保持宋、明以来街市格局，现划为重点保护的历史街区。

*PROTECTION OF THE ANCIENT CITY*

*In 1986, the State Council issued an instruction concerning the protection of the ancient Suzhou, giving special emphasis to "the old city proper", "the two routes" (from Shantang Canal and Street, Shangtang Canal and Street, to Fengqiao Road), and "the three scenic areas (the West Garden and Lingering Garden, the Town of Maple Bridge, and the Tiger Hill). The water alley along Pingjiang Street is a major historical area of protection in the northeastern section of the ancient city, where houses face the street in front and adjoin the canal in the rear, maintaining the traditional urban form since the Song and Ming Dynasties.*

平江水巷 *The water alley along Pingjiang Street.*

山塘街、河 *Shantang Street and Canal*

上塘街、河 *Shangtang Street and Canal*

## 山塘街、河

位于阊门外。与名胜虎丘相连，为唐白居易所筑，亦称“白公堤”。

*SHANTANG STREET AND CANAL*

*Outside Changmen Gate, the canal and the street along it, also called the Causeway of Lord Bai, which lead to the Tiger Hill, were constructed under the command of Bai Juyi of the Tang Dynasty.*

## 上塘街、河

位于阊门外。通向枫桥、寒山寺的旧道。明清时，街上店铺林立，河内舟楫比肩。

*SHANGTANG STREET AND CANAL*

*Outside Changmen Gate, they are the traditional access to Maple Bridge and Han Shan Temple. Shops used to line the street and water traffic was busy during the Ming and Qing period.*

湖心亭 *The Mid-lake Pavilion.*

### 西园寺 ●●

位于阊门外，为江南著名古刹。始建于元代，初名归元寺，明崇祯八年（1635年）改名戒幢律寺，俗称西园寺。寺内佛像造型生动传神。

*WEST GARDEN MONASTERY*

*Located outside Changmen Gate and famous throughout the southern Yangtze Delta, the monastery was first built in the Yuan Dynasty with the name, Guiyuan Monastery. It assumed the name, the Monastery of Prohibition and Discipline, in the 8th year of Chongzhen Reign of the Ming (1635 AD), popularly called West Garden Monastery. It is most famous for its vivid and lifelike Buddhist statues.*

罗汉堂 *The Hall of Arhats.*

寒山寺塔 *The Han Shan Pagoda.*

## 寒山寺

位于城西枫桥古镇。始建于南朝梁天监年间，初名“妙利普明塔院”。相传唐代高僧寒山、拾得曾云游至此，遂易名寒山寺。因唐张继《枫桥夜泊》诗名扬海内外。

*HAN SHAN TEMPLE*

*In the ancient Fengqiao Town, it was first built during the Tian Jian Reign of the Liang of Southern Dynasties with the original name as Miaolipuming Pagoda Court. It is popularly believed that the famous monks Han Shan and Shi De once stayed here in their travel. Hence the name. Its reputation was greatly boosted by the Tang poet Zhang Ji's verse "Night Mooring at Maple Bridge".*

钟楼 *The Bell Tower.*

铁铃关 *The Iron Bell Pass.*



## 铁铃关

位于寒山寺畔。建于明嘉靖三十六年（1557年），为明抗倭史迹，与枫桥、古运河组成苏州城西的一道重要屏障。

*THE IRON BELL PASS*

*In the vicinity of Han Shan Temple, it was built in the 36th year of Jiajing Reign of the Ming (1557 AD) as a fortress against Japanese pirates, and it joins with the Grand Canal and Maple Bridge to form a vital pass in the west of the city.*

## 江村桥

位于寒山寺前，横跨枫江，与枫桥遥遥相对，古桥宝刹，别具风致。

*JIANGCUN BRIDGE*

*In front of Han Shan Temple and spanning Maple Canal and overlooking Maple Bridge, this ancient bridge matches the old temple in a harmonious scene.*

江村桥 *The Jiangcun Bridge.*

虎丘塔　（五代）

*The Tiger Hill Pagoda (from the Period of Five Dynasties).*

## 虎　丘

又名海涌山。位于阊门外。传春秋吴王阖闾葬此后三日，有白虎蹲其上，故名虎丘。古塔殿阁因山就势布局得宜；树木葱茏，山石峭奇，而成佳境；为“吴中第一名胜”。苏东坡有“到苏州不游虎丘乃憾事也”之说。

## *THE TIGER HILL*

*Located outside Changmen Gate and also known as Hanyong Hill, it was named the Tiger Hill from the legend that a white tiger appeared crouching on the hill three days after the burial of the King He Lu of Wu State in the Spring and Autumn Period. Buildings and the pagoda are scattered along the natural slope of the hill amidst luxuriant verdure and sheer cliffs and grotesque rocks, and the place is reputed as the No. 1 sight in the Wu Region. The poet Su Dongpo once remarked, "It is a loss to visit Suzhou without seeing the Tiger Hill."*

虎丘摩崖石刻（唐至清）●

*Engravings on the cliffs of the Tiger Hill (from the Tang to the Qing Dynasties).*

京杭大运河 *Beijing-Hangzhou Grand Canal*

横塘驿亭 *Messenger Station at Hengtang*

### 京杭大运河

历史上是苏州通向外埠的大动脉，经整治保存完好。

### *BEIJING-HANGZHOU GRAND CANAL*

*It is a transportation artery in Suzhou's history, and now in excellent preservation after renovation and dredging.*

### 横塘驿亭

在古城西南部，京杭大运河畔，是中国现存最早的邮亭。

### *MESSENGER STATION AT HENGTANG*

*On the southwestern part of the city, it is the earliest postal station being preserved in China.*

## 宝带桥 ●●

位于城东南大运河畔。始建于唐元和十一至十四年（816-819年），宋、明、清重建。全长317米，有53个石拱孔。

## *PRECIOUS BELT BRIDGE*

*On the Grand Canal in the southeast of the city, it was first built from the 11th to 14th year of Yuan He Reign of the Tang Dynasty (816-819 AD) and reconstructed in the Song, Ming, and Qing Dynasties with 53 arches and total length of 317 meters.*

观前街 *Guanqian Street.*

## 古城更新

古城内留有旧房大多建于清至民国年代，年久失修。近年在保护有价值的传统民居和传统街巷风貌原则下，逐步实施古城街坊的更新改造。古城内新建住房严格控制高度与体量，配置现代生活设施，呈现浓郁的地方特色风貌。

*New Look of the Ancient City*

*Since most of the old houses in the city proper, dating from the Qing and Period of the Republic, are in a bad state of repair, renovation and transformation have been grudually carried out in old street blocks in recent years under the principle of protecting those houses of historical values and maintaining the traditional style of the streets forms. All the newly built houses within the ancient city proper, strictly limited in heights and capacities according to official regulations, are equipped with modern facilities and retain architectural styles of strong local flavor.*

十全街水巷 *The canal behind Shiquan Street.*

古城新巷 *A new alley in the ancient city.*

桐芳苑 *The housing estate of Tongfang Garden.*

干将路 *Ganjiang Road*

南浩街与环城河 *Nanhao Street along the moat.*

贰

古典园林

CLASSICAL GARDENS

香洲

*The Isle of Fragrance*

见山楼 *The Tower of Mountain View.*

## 拙政园

位于东北街。明御史王献臣建园，取晋潘岳《闲赋居》中“拙者为政”之意，故名拙政园。园分东、中、西三部分，水面开阔，布局疏朗，建筑多对景、借景佳作，是江南古典园林的代表作。

## *THE HUMBLE ADMINISTRATOR'S GARDEN*

*On Dongbei Street, it was built by Wang Xianchen, an imperial censor of the Ming Dynasty. The garden derived its name from the idea of "the politics of a humble administrator" in the essay, "On Life of Leisure", by Pan Yue of the Jin Dynasty. It is divided into the eastern, central, and western sections with spacious ponds in a style of openness. Landscaping techniques of contrast and borrowed views are used to provide varied prospects in the garden, which is a typical example of the classical gardens in the southern Yangtze Delta.*

小飞虹 *The Small Rainbow Bridge.*

水廊 *The water-side corridor.*

芙蓉榭 *The Lotus Pavilion.*

冠云峰 *The Cloud-Crowned Peak.*

## 留 园

位于阊门外。始建于明万历年间。园内建筑布置精巧，引人入胜。园中冠云峰为北宋花石纲遗物，是江南最大的湖石奇峰之一。

*THE LINGERING GARDEN*

*Located outside Changmen Gate, it was created in Wanli Reign of the Ming with most attractive architectural forms and elaborate furnishings. The Cloud-crowned Peak in the garden, which was left from the famous imperial tribute "Huashigang", is the largest single piece of Tai Lake rock in the area south of the Yangtze.*

鸳鸯厅 *The Hall of Mandarin-ducks.*

五峰仙馆 *The Immortal's Hall of Five Peaks.*

明瑟楼 *The Tower of Crystal Waters.*

## 网师园

位于十全街。原为南宋史正志万卷堂故址。园内建筑互为因借，花木经意栽植。中部亭台轩榭围绕池水而造，园虽小而意境无穷。

## *THE MASTER-OF-NETS GARDEN*

*On Shiquan Street, it was originally the Hall of Book Volumes, the former residence of Shi Zhengzhi of the Southern Song Dynasty. The buildings in the garden are artfully laid out to complement each other, while trees and flowers are selected with*

月到风来亭、看松读画轩 *The Pavilion of Moon-lit Night an*

*critical taste, and the pavilions, terraces, and halls in the central part are spread out around a central pool to create great depth of perspective in a limited space.*

竹外一枝轩、射鸭廊、半山亭

*The Bamboo-fringed Pavilion, Duck Hunting Corridor and Half-hill Pavilion.*

洞壑 *The mountain caves.*

## 环秀山庄

位于景德路。原为五代金谷园故址。园内假山峥嵘峭拔、气势雄伟，峰回路转、变化无穷，系清乾、嘉年间叠山名家戈裕良之作。

*THE MOUNTAIN VILLA OF SECLUDED BEAUTY*

*Located on the former site of the Garden of Golden Grains of the Five Dynasties period on Jingde Road, the garden is focused on an intricate and towering artificial hill, created by the master rockery designer Ge Yuliang during Qian Long and Jia Qing Reigns of the Qing.*

山水相依 *The mountain peaks over waters.*

沧浪亭外景 *The Surging Waves Pavilion viewed from the outside.*



## 沧浪亭

位于人民路南端。苏州最古老园林之一。五代为孙承祐别墅，北宋归苏舜钦。园邻广阔水面，园内亭筑高丘，竹树笼翠，景色雅致。

*THE SURGING WAVES PAVILION*

*Located on the southern section of Renmin Road, it is the oldest classical garden in Suzhou, first built in the period of Five Dynasties as Sun Chengyou's villa, then the home of Su Shunqin in the Northern Song Dynasty. The garden is fronted by a expansive water of a canal, and pavilions inside are built on hilltops surrounded by trees and bamboo groves in luxuriant verdure.*

沧浪亭 *The Pavilion of Surging Waves.*

**狮子林**

位于园林路。始建于元至正二年（1342年），园中湖石假山多呈狮子状，故名。园内建筑精美，山壑宛转，变化迷离。

*THE LION GROVE GARDEN*

*On Yuanlin Road, the garden was built in the 2nd year of Zhi Zheng Reign of the Yuan Dynasty (1342 AD). It is so named because many of the Taihu rocks in the garden bear the resemblance of lions. The garden is characterized by exquisite buildings and a labyrinth of mountain paths and grottos.*

## 耦　园

位于小新桥巷。清初陆锦所筑，同治年沈秉成扩建，是典型的水乡第宅园林。园分东西，以黄石假山见长，配以重檐厅楼，幽曲有趣。

*THE GARDEN OF COUPLE'S RETREAT*

*Located in Xiaoxinqiao Alley, it was first built by Lu Jing in the early Qing period, later expaned by Shen Bingcheng during Tongzhi Reign as a typical private residential garden in the water country. Divided into eastern and western parts, the garden excels in the artificial hill piled with yellow granite rocks surrounded by double-eave towers and halls in a tranquil setting.*

听橹楼 *The Hall of Splashing Oars.*

山水间 *Amidst mountains and waters.*

## 艺　圃

位于文衙弄。明嘉靖年间袁祖庚始建。园以池水居中，池北亭榭参差，池南假山林立，风格质朴自然，颇多山林野趣。乳鱼亭、博雅堂均为明代原物。

*THE GARDEN OF HERB CULTIVATION*

*In Wenya Lane, the garden was built by Yuan Zugeng in Jia Jing Reign of the Ming. Pavilions and halls are concentrated on the north of the central pond, overlooking the groups of rocks in the south, giving off a simple, rustic flavor of mountain forest. Among the buildings, the Pavilion of Feeding Fish and the Hall of Antiquity belong to the original architecture of the Ming Period.*

## 怡　园

位于人民路中段。原为明尚书吴宽旧宅，清同治十三年（1874年）顾文彬建园，名取怡情悦性之意。园仿苏州各园妙景而筑，饶有情趣。

## *THE GARDEN OF HARMONY*

*On the middle section of Renmin Road, it used to be the home of Wu Kuan, a minister of the Ming. In the 10th year of Tong Chi Reign of the Qing (1874 AD), Gu Wenbin built this elegant garden by taking over the fine elements of other gardens in Suzhou and named it to express the idea of harmony of the pleased mind.*

五峰园 （明） *The Garden of Five Pines (of the Ming Dynasty).*

北半园 （清） *The Northern Half Garden (of the Qing Dynasty).*

听枫园 （清） *The Garden of Whispering Maples (of the Qing Dynasty).*

# 叁 太湖名胜

FAMOUS SIGHTS ON LAKE TAI

太湖帆影

*Sail boats on Lake Tai.*

轩辕宫正殿 （元）
*The main hall of Xuanyuan Palace (of the Yuan Dynasty).*

## 洞庭东山

山为太湖半岛，风景如画。西卯坞有唐代所建紫金庵，庵内泥塑为宋代雕塑名手雷潮夫妇所作；上湾有明善堂；此外还有翁巷的启园、杨湾的轩辕宫等。

## *EAST DONGTING HILL*

*A picturesque peninsular in Lake Tai, it is known for scenic spots, chiefly the Purple Gold Nunnery built in the Tang Dynasty, in which are preserved the clay sculptures of Buddhist Arhats by the hand of the famous sculptor Lei Chao and his wife, The Hall of Benevolence in Shangwan, Qiyuan Garden in Wengxiang, and Xuanyuan Palace in Yangwan, etc.*

明善堂 （明） *The Hall of Benevolence (of the Ming Dynasty).*

紫金庵罗汉塑像 （宋）
*A clay statue in Purple Gold Nunnery (of the Song Dynasty).*

启园 （1933年） *Qiyuan Garden (built in 1933).*

柳毅井及碑 （明）

*Liu Yi Well and the inscribed stone stele (of the Ming Dynasty).*

雕花楼 （1922年） *The Carved Mansion.*

## 洞庭西山

太湖中最大的岛屿。岛南石公山伸向湖内，与湖中三山岛遥相呼应，构成一幅绮丽的天然山水画。岛中林屋洞内立石成林，洞顶如屋平整，为道教天下第九洞天。明湾、东村等古建筑以及梅花、桔树等值得一赏。

## *WEST DONGTING HILL*

*It is the largest island in Lake Tai. Shigong Hill on the southern tip extends into the great lake, overlooking Sanshan Island in the distance to present a spectacular panorama of mountains and waters. In the island there is Linwu Cave, in which staglites stand like a forest under smooth ceilings, acclaimed by Taoist believers as No. 9 Cave under Heaven. The island is also famous for the ancient buildings in Mingwan and Dongcun, and the scenes of plum blossoms and tangerine groves.*

石公山 *Shigong Hill.*

西山梅园 *Plum blossoms in West Hill.*

太湖人家 *Dwellings on the shores of Lake Tai.*

植里古道及桥 *The ancient pathway and Bridge in Zhili.*

林屋洞 *Linwu Cave.*

西施玩花池 *Flower Pond of Xi Shi.*

## 灵岩山

位于城西南木渎镇畔。以千姿百态的嶙峋奇石、众多的春秋时吴宫遗迹、历史悠久的佛教胜地闻名遐迩。

*LINGYAN HILL*

*Located near Mudu Township to the southwest of Suzhou, the hill is noted for its peaks in multifarious shapes, the historical remains from the resort palace of Wu State in the Spring and Autumn Period, and the time-honored Buddhist sanctuary.*

灵岩山寺 （宋至民国） *Lingyan Hill Monastery (from the Song to the Period of the Republic).*

## 天平山

位于城西15公里。以怪石、清泉、红枫“三绝”著称，还因其与宋代名臣范仲淹史迹紧密相连而名扬四海。

*TIANPING HILL*

*15 kilometers to the west of Suzhou city, the hill is wellknown for the "three unique scenes": grotesque rocks, limped springs, and red maples. The famous historical relics on the hill are closely associated with the great civil servant Fan Zhongyan of the Song Dynasty.*

天平红枫 *The red maples on Tianping Hill.*

一线天 *A Strip of Sky.*

穹窿日出 *Sunrise over Conglong Mountain.*

上真观 *Shangzhen Taoist Temple.*

## 穹窿山

位于城西25公里。山上人文景观甚多，著名的有孙武苑、上真观、宁邦寺、百丈泉、御碑亭等。全山林木深秀，景色迷人，为东吴国家森林公园。

*CONGLONG MOUNTAIN*

*25 kilometers to the west of the city, the hill abounds in spots of historical interest, the most famous being Sun Wu Garden, Shangzhen Temple, Ningbang Monastery, the Tall Spring, and the Pavilion of Imperial Tablet, etc. Covered with beautiful green woods, the hill has been officially listed as Dongwu National Forest Park.*

## 天池山

位于城西约20公里。山上有池，池畔顽石天成，池水清彻。池畔有元建寂鉴寺，还有钵盂泉、莲花峰等胜迹。

### *TIANCHI HILL*

*20 kilometers to the west of the city, the hill is named Heavenly Pool on account of the natural lake rimmed with huge rocks around. By the pool lie Jijian Monastery and other scenic spots such as Bowl Spring and Lotus Peak.*

天池山 *Tianchi Hill*

华山摩崖石刻 *Engraved inscription on the cliffs of Huashan Hill.*

## 华　山

距城西约20公里。山道险峻，多象形奇石与摩崖石刻，有“吴中第一大佛”、“五十三参”、翠岩寺、御碑等胜景。

### *HUASHAN HILL*

*About 20 kilometers to the west of the city, the hill is accessed by steep path between sheer cliffs and rocks of all shapes. The tourist spots include "No. 1 Buddha in the Wu region", "Fifty-three pilgrimages", Cuiyan Temple, and the Stone Tablet of Imperial Inscription, etc.*

## 石　湖

为太湖的分支与内湾，因湖底皆石故名。春秋时，石湖山水是吴王游赏之苑囿，又是吴越相争之战场。有茶磨屿、范成大祠、渔庄等胜景。明代起，民间有八月十八日“石湖串月”活动流传至今。

## *STONE LAKE*

*A tributary bay of Lake Tai, the lake is so called because it has a rocky bottom. In the Spring and Autumn Period, the kings of Wu State used to build their royal resorts here, and battles were also fought here between the states of Wu and Yue. Places of interest in this area include Chamo isle, the Shrine of Fan Chengda, and the Yu Villa. A folk custom has been alive since the Ming Dynasty to "make excursion to the Stone Lake to Watch the moon" on every 18th day of the 8th lunar month.*

上方山楞伽塔（宋） *Lengjia Pagoda on Shangfang Hill (of the Song).*

行春桥、越城桥 （清重建） *Hangchun Bridge and Yuecheng Bridge (rebuilt in the Qing).*

范成大祠 （明清） *The Shrine of Fan Chengda (the Ming and Qing period).*

渔庄（1934年） *The Yu Villa (built in 1934).*

万佛石塔 *The Stone Stupa of Ten Thousand Buddhas.*

## 万佛石塔

位于镇湖镇西泾村，始建于宋。通体用青石砌成，塔内壁雕有万余佛像，故称万佛石塔。

*THE STONE STUPA OF TEN THOUSAND BUDDHAS*

*A gray granite stone stupa built in the Song Dynasty in Xijing Village, Zhenhu Township, its inside walls are carved with over ten thousand images of Buddha, hence the name.*

## 邓尉山

位于光福镇境内。传东汉光武帝时太尉邓禹隐居此山故名。留有邓禹手植、被清帝乾隆誉为“清、奇、古、怪”古柏四棵（见右页）。“清”，孤高伟岸；“奇”，雷劈分叉；“古”，绕曲古拙；“怪”，雷击偃伏。此山“香雪海”为我国四大探梅胜地之一。

*DENG WEI HILL*

*Located in the township of Guangfu, it is where Deng Wei, a cabinet minister in the Guang Wu Reign of the Eastern Han Dynasty retired to live in his respite, hence the name of the hill. The four cypress trees planted by Deng Wei have survived to this day, named by Emperor Qianlong of the Qing "Pure" (solitary and upright), "Odd" (split in half by a thunderbolt), "Antique" (twisted and coiling in age), and "Grotesque" (alive from the thunder-struck trunk). The area is one of the four great scenic spots for plum blossoms in China.*

清 *The Pure.*

古 *The Antique.*

奇 *The Odd.*

怪 *The Grotesque.*

双桥夜色

*The night view of the Double Bridges.*

## 周　庄

位于苏城西南约30多公里处。宋元祐元年（1086年），周迪功郎在此设庄故名。前街后河，颇多拱桥、踏级。茶楼酒肆夹桥而立，屋檐马头高低错落，显示出典型的江南水乡风貌。为江苏省历史文化名镇。

### *ZHOUZHUANG TOWNSHIP*

*About 30 kilometers to the southwest of Suzhou city, the township was named after Zhou Digong, who first built his villa house here in the 1st year of Yuan You Reign of the Song (1086). Canals extend along the back of streets, crossed by arched bridges with stone steps, where teahouses and restaurants hang over the waters. The traditional houses with upturned eaves stand at varying heights. All this makes a typical scene of the water-bound town in the southern Yangtze Delta. It has been declared a town of historical and cultural fame in Jiangsu Province.*

富安桥　（元）　*Fu'an Bridge (of the Yuan).*

过街楼巷 *The alley with an overpass tower.*

迷楼 *Milou, the two-story chamber.*

沈厅 *The Hall of the Shens.*

## 同　里

位于苏城东南约18公里处。五湖环抱，河道纵横；有耕乐堂、退思园等名宅名园。白墙黛瓦、花木掩映，洋溢出一片水乡柔情。为江苏省历史文化名镇。

## *TONGLI TOWNSHIP*

*18 kilometers to the southeast of Suzhou city, the township is surrounded by five lakes and crossed by numerous waterways. Among the famous gardens and residential houses are the Hall of Happy Tillers and the Garden of Meditation. White walls, dark roof-tiles, flowers and trees adorn the typical setting of the water country. It is one of the towns of historical and cultural fame in Jiangsu Province.*

三桥 *The Triple Bridges.*

古宅　*An old home.*

旧弄　*An old-fashioned alley.*

古镇雪景 *The ancient township after snowfall.*

退思园 （清） *The Garden of Meditation (of the Qing).*

罗星洲 *Luoxing Isle.*

水道驳岸 （宋至清） *The waterway embankment (from the Song to the Qing).*

## 甪 直

位于苏城东南约18公里处，古称甫里。南朝梁始建保圣寺，留存唐代彩塑和斗鸭池等。小河、小街、小桥与水乡女子、农家服饰独具风韵。为江苏省历史文化名镇。

*LUZHI TOWNSHIP*

*18 kilometers to the southeast of Suzhou city and originally called Puli, the township is well-known for its ancient streets, canals, bridges, and the country women's traditional costumes, apart from the glamorous Baosheng Monastery, built in the Liang Dynasty during the period of Southern Dynasties, in which are preserved the colored clay statues of the Tang Dynasty and the Duck-fighting Pond, etc. It is currently on the list of towns of historical and cultural fame in Jiangsu Province.*

保圣寺罗汉塑像 （唐）

*Statues of Arhats in Baosheng Monastery (of the Tang).*

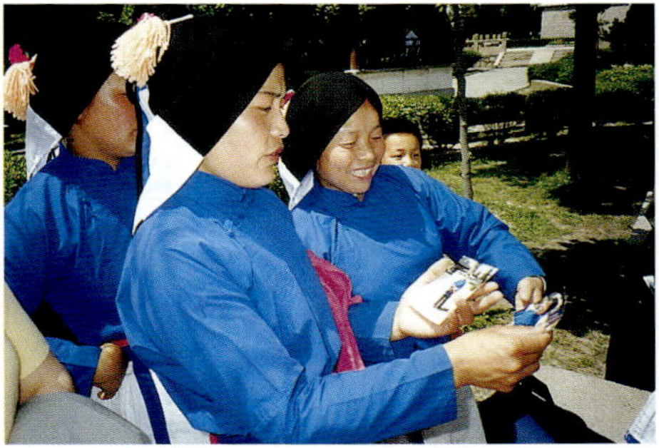

水乡服饰 *Folk costume of the water country.*

水韵
The rhythm of water.

河棚 *An archway along the canal.*

廊桥 *A covered bridge.*

## 木 渎

位于苏州城西约10公里。传春秋时吴王夫差在灵岩山建“馆娃宫”，运来的木材“木塞于渎”，得名木渎。镇内河道纵横，街巷古朴，建筑精巧，古迹颇多，誉称园林古镇。为江苏省历史文化名镇。

*MUDU TOWNSHIP*

*About 10 kilometers to the west of Suzhou city, the town dates back to the Spring and Autumn Period, when King of Wu State had timber transported to the nearby Lingyan Hill to build his resort palace and later left so much timber here that it "blocked the waterway" and subsequently a town was built with it. Listed as a town of historical and cultural fame of Jiangsu Province, Mudu is reputed as an ancient town of gardens, with a great number of waterways, old streets, exquisite buildings, and cultural relics.*

冯桂芬故居 *The former residence of Feng Guifeng.*

严家花园 *The Garden of the Yans.*

深巷塔影 *A looming pagoda through a deep, narrow alley.*

## 光　福

位于苏州城西约20多公里的太湖之滨。南朝梁大同年间，顾氏舍宅建光福寺，遂以寺名镇。镇内层峦迭翠，邓尉山梅林似海，山水间充满诗情画意。为江苏省历史文化名镇。

## *GUANGFU TOWNSHIP*

*Located on the shores of Lake Tai about 20 kilometers to the west of Suzhou city, the town is named after Guangfu Monastery, which was built on the site of the Gu's donated home in the Reign of Da Tong of Liang Dynasty. As one of the towns of historical and cultural fame in Jiangsu Province, the town is surrounded by picturesque hills and Lake Tai, the most famous being Deng Wei Hill, where one can feast the eye on a sea of plum blossoms.*

香雪海 （清） *The Pavilion of Sea of Snowy Fragrance (of the Qing).*

铜观音寺前宋桥 （宋）

*The Song Dynasty bridge in front of the Temple of Merciful Goddess.*

光福寺塔 （宋） *The Pagoda of Guangfu Monastery (of the Song).*

小王山摩崖石刻 （现代）
*The inscriptions on the cliff of Xiaowang Hill (of modern times).*

## 藏 书

位于苏州城西。因西汉名臣朱买臣在此筑楼藏书得名。境内穹窿、天池、华山等风光旖旎，名胜古迹遍布。藏书艺人生产的澄泥砚为全国四大名砚之一，藏书羊肉风味闻名江南。

*CANGSHU TOWNSHIP*

*To the west of Suzhou city, the town got its name, Cangshu (meaning "storing books"), from the fact that the famous civil servant Zhu Maichen of the Western Han Dynasty once built his library here. There are many scenic spots and cultural relics within its boundaries, such as Conglong Mountain, Tianchi Hill and Huashan Hill. The carved Chengni stone ink slabs made by the local craftsmen are one of the four most valued varieties in China. The local cuisine of mutton feast is popular throughout the southern Yangtze Delta.*

小桥流水人家 *The houses along a canal with bridges.*

三羊开泰 *The good omen of three goats.*

## 黄 埭

位于苏城西北。始建于春秋时期。战国时楚国名相春申君黄歇兴修水利，筑成堰埭，名春申埭，故后称黄埭。自然条件优越，近年来外企增多，经济实力大大加强。

*HUANGDAI TOWNSHIP*

*To the northwest of Suzhou, the town derived its name from a dam in the water conservancy project initialed by Huang Xie, the Lord of Chun Shen in the Spring and Autumn Period. Bestowed with advantageous natural conditions, the town has in recent years attracted more and more investors from the outside and its economy has grown considerably.*

漕湖夕照 *Sunset over Caohu Lake.*

黄歇雕像 *The sculpture of Huang Xie.*

枕河人家. *Dwellings along a canal.*

干将坊
*The memorial archway for Gan Jiang.*

## 伍子胥（？-前484年）

名员。春秋楚国人，因避祸逃吴，得吴王阖闾重用，建阖闾大城，即今苏州古城。其重视水利，开有胥溪、胥浦。今存胥门、胥口、胥山及位于盘门的伍相祠等纪念地。

*WU ZIXU (?-484 BC)*

*Wu Yuan, a native and refugee from the state of Chu, won the trust of King He Lu of Wu State, and was appointed to command the construction of the Great City of He Lu, which is today's Suzhou city. He made endeavors to build water conservancy works and dug canals of Xuxi and Xupu. Memorial buildings for him can be found today in Xumen Gate, Xukou, Xushan Hill, and the Shrine of Prime Minister Wu at Panmen Gate.*

伍员像 *The portrait of Wu Yuan.*

伍相祠 *The Shrine of Prime Minister Wu.*

## 孙　武（生卒年不详）

字长卿，春秋齐国人。因战乱避奔吴国。经伍子胥向吴王举荐，为吴将，与伍子胥一起“西破强楚”、“北威齐晋”。留有《孙子兵法》13篇，为世人传诵。穹窿山有孙武子隐居地、兵圣堂等胜迹。

## *SUN WU*

*(Dates of birth and death undetermined)*

*Sun Wu, also named Changqing, was a native of Qi State and while taking refuge from war in Wu State, he was recommended to the king of Wu by Wu Zixu to take up military command. Working closely with Wu Zixu, he led the Wu troops to "capture the Chu State in the west" and "defeat the states of Qi and Jin in the north". The 13 chapters of his classic work, the Art of War, are still being studied throughout the world. There are relics of his hermitage and the Hall of Military Sage in Conglong Mountain.*

孙武像 *The portrait of Sun Wu.*

孙武子隐居地 *The site of Sun Wu's hermitage.*

朱买臣读书台（汉） *The terrace where Zhu Maichen used to study.*

## 朱买臣（？-前115年）

字翁子。吴县人，汉代辞赋家。家贫好学，以儒学文词名于当时。汉武帝时被擢为中大夫，后拜会稽太守（郡治今苏州）。穹窿山东麓有其读书台。

## *ZHU MAICHEN (?-115 BC)*

*Zhu Maichen, or Wengzi by grown-up name, an essayist in the Han Dynasty, was born of a poor family and became well-known for his Confucian study and literature. During the Reign of Wudi, he was appointed to official posts, and at one time, he was the prefect of Guiji (with office in today's Suzhou). A relic of his study can be found in the eastern slope of Conglong Mountain.*

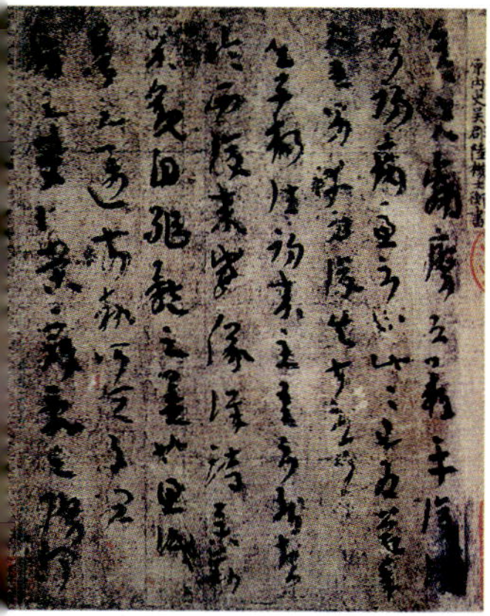

平复帖 · 陆机
*The calligraphical work "Pingfu" by Luji.*

## 陆　机（261-303年）

字士衡。为东吴名将陆逊之孙，书法家、文学家。自幼读书为文，才华横溢，著有《文赋》、《干山子》等，有“文贵创新”见解，对中国文学发展有积极影响。

*LUJI (261-303 AD)*

*Luji, Shiheng by grown-up name, the grandson of Lu Xun of Dongwu State and a calligrapher and literary figure, proved his literary talent since early childhood. His works "Wenfu" and "Ganshanzi", and the idea, "originality is the soul of literary creation", exerted positive impact on the development of Chinese literature.*

陆机像 *The portrait of Luji.*

## 陆龟蒙（？-约881年）

字鲁望，唐代著名诗人。长洲（今苏州）人。举进士不中，后隐居甫里（现角直），自号甫里先生。常泛舟太湖，吟诗作赋，与皮日休为友，世称“皮陆”。角直镇留有其遗迹斗鸭池等。

*LU GUIMENG (?-around 881 AD)*

*Lu Guimeng, Luwang by adult name, an accomplished poet in the Tang Dynasty, was born in Changzhou (today's Suzhou). After his repeated failures in civil examinations, he led a hermit's life in Fuli (today's Luzhi) and named himself "Scholar Fuli". He was often seen sailing on Lake Tai composing poems and spent much of his time with his friend Pi Rixiiu. The two poets later referred to as "Pi and Lu". Photo shows one of the relics about him, the Duck-fighting Pond.*

斗鸭池 *The Duck-fighting Pond.*

范仲淹像
*The portrait of Fan Zhongyan.*

## 范仲淹（989-1052年）

字希文，苏州人。北宋著名政治家、文学家、军事家。景佑元年（1034年）任苏州知州，办府学，兴水利，置义庄，政绩卓著。有“先天下之忧而忧，后天下之乐而乐”名句流传千古。

## *FAN ZHONGYAN (989-1052 AD)*

*A native of Suzhou and Xiwen by adult name, Fan was a great statesmen, literary figure, and military strategist in the Northern Song Dynasty. After he took office as prefect of Suzhou in the 1st year of Jing You Reign (1034 AD), he exercised meritorious administration of the area by founding the prefecture school, improving the flood diversion project, and establishing charity institutions. His famous saying, "Be the first to worry the woes of the people, and the last to share the weal of the people", has become the classic motto for generation after generation.*

府学大成殿 （宋） *The Hall of Confucius in prefecture school (of the Song).*

## 葛可久（1305-1353年）

名乾孙，苏州人。元代医学家。精于医理，博采各家所长，疑难杂症应手而愈。著有《十药神书》等医书，对吴门医派的形成，颇具影响。

*GE KEJIU (1305-1353 AD)*

*Ge Kejiu, also named Qian Sun, was a great physician of the Yuan Dynasty, who absorbed the fine elements of various schools of Chinese medicine and cured many hard diseases. His medical work, "Book of Ten Prescriptions", promoted the growth of Wu School of Medicine.*

葛可久像 *The portrait of Ge Kejiu.*

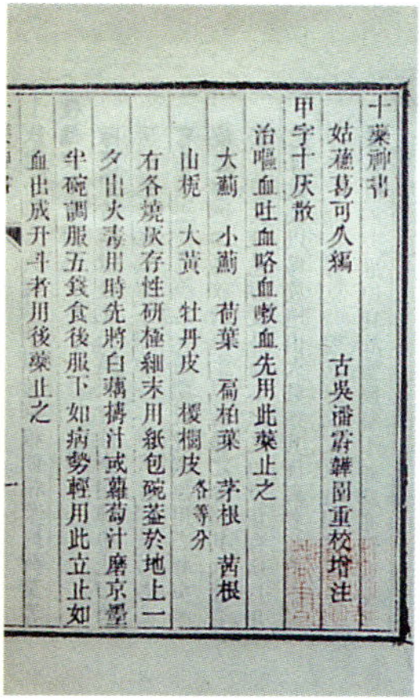

十藥神書

姑蘇葛可久編　古吳潘霨韡園重校增注

甲字十灰散

治嘔血吐血咯血嗽血先用此藥止之

大薊　小薊　荷葉　扁柏葉　茅根　茜根

山梔　大黃　牡丹皮　棕櫚皮　各等分

右各燒灰存性研極細末用紙包碗蓋於地上一夕出火毒用時先將白藕擣汁或蘿蔔汁磨京墨半碗調服五錢食後服下如病勢輕用此立止如血出成升斗者用後藥止之

《十药神书》 *The Book of Ten Prescriptions.*

蒯祥像
*The bust of Kuai Xiang.*

## 蒯　祥（1398-1481年）

明代杰出的建筑大师。吴县香山人。参与北京天安门、故宫三大殿、十三陵之裕陵等重大工程的规划建设。官至工部左侍郎，有“蒯鲁班”之称。

蒯祥墓　（明） *The tomb of Kuai Xiang.*

*KUAI XIANG (1398-1481 AD)*

*An outstanding architect born in Xiangshan, Suzhou, in the Ming Dynasty, Kuai Xiang played a major role in the planning and construction of Tian An Men Gate, the three main halls of the Imperial Palace, and the Ming Tombs in Beijing. He rose to the position of vice-minister of industry and was popularly called the "Incarnation of Lu Ban", the legendary craftsman.*

顾炎武像 *The portrait of Gu Yanwu .*

## 顾炎武（1613-1682年）

明末清初杰出的思想家、爱国学者。其“天下兴亡，匹夫有责”的至理名言为世人传诵。著作有《日知录》、《音乐五书》等。现昆山市有为纪念其而命名的亭林园、顾炎武纪念馆等。

*GU YANWU (1613-1682 AD)*

*A great thinker and patriotic scholar at the end of the Ming and in the early Qing period, he is remembered by the Chinese people for his monitorial remark, "When the fate of the nation is at stake, it is the duty of every ordinary citizen to save the country from peril." He was the author of "Record of Daily Awareness", "Music in Five Series", and other books. Tinglin Park and the Memorial Hall of Gu Yanwu have been built in his memory in Kunshan.*

## 叶圣陶（1894-1988年）

苏州人。著名教育家、作家等。1921年与茅盾、郑振铎等组织“文学研究会”，为“五四”新文学运动先驱者之一。从事教育工作70余年，写有大量专著。曾任第六届全国政协副主席等职。甪直镇有叶圣陶执教旧址、纪念馆等。

*YE SHENGTAO (1894-1988 AD)*

*A native of Suzhou and well-known educationist and writer, Ye organized "Society of Literary Studies" with Mao Dun and Zheng Zhenduo. He was one the pioneers of the May 4th New Literature Movement, and devoted to the cause of education for over 70 years with many theoretical works. He once held the position of vice-chairman of the 6th National People's Political Consultative Conference. The site of his teaching activities and a memorial hall are being preserved in Luzhi Township.*

叶圣陶纪念馆 *Memorial Hall of Ye Shengtao.*

东园图（局部）· 文徵明
*The painting, "East Garden" (in part) by Wen Zhenming.*

孟蜀宫妓图 · 唐寅

*"The Courtesans at Meng Shu's Royal Palace" by Tang Yin.*

## 吴门画派

吴门画派崛起于明代中叶，代表人物有沈周、文徵明、唐寅和仇英。其作品开创了一代新风，在中国画坛产生深远影响。

### *WU SCHOOL OF PAINTING*

*The mid-Ming Dynasty saw the rise of Wu School of Painting, chiefly represented by artists Shen Zhou, Wen Zhenming, Tang Yin, and Qiu Ying. The school opened up a new trail and had far-reaching influence upon the art of Chinese painting.*

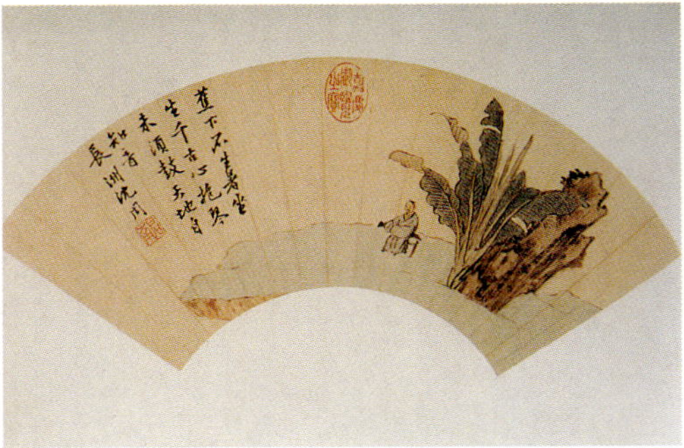

蕉阴琴思 · 沈周

*"Lute Music under the Shade of Banana Trees" by Shen Zhou.*

虎踞龙盘 （清）
*The Crouching Tiger and Coiling Dragon (from the Qing).*

云蒸霞蔚 （清） *The Sunlight through Clouds (from the Qing).*

秦汉遗韵 （明）
*The Lingering Flavor of the Qin and Han Times (from the Ming).*



## 苏派盆景

我国盆景艺术主要流派之一。有古雅拙朴、取法自然、耐人寻味的特点。自宋代起绵延流传，现代有周瘦鹃、朱子安等高手。在国内历届展赛中，苏派盆景屡获殊荣。

## *SUZHOU-STYLE POTTED LANDSCAPE*

*It is one of the main schools in the Chinese art of potted landscape, and has the special features of antique look, natural shaping, and expressive for contemplation. With its origin in the Song period, the art has been developing continuously to this day, with modern representatives like the master hands Zhou Shoujuan and Zhu Zi'an. Landscape pots from Suzhou have won many an award in national exhibitions.*

## 评　弹

用苏州方言进行说唱表演的地方曲种。源头可追溯到唐代的变文和说唱文学，大致形成于明末清初。其说噱变幻有趣，唱腔婉转清丽，历代流派甚多。

## *SUZHOU BALLAD SINGING*

*A folk art of story-telling in narrative and singing in Suzhou local dialect, this form of art originated from the story-telling and singing literature of the Tang Dynasty, and matured in the late Ming and early Qing Dynasties. The story-telling is full of witticism and humor, while the singing is mellow and melodious. Various styles of presentation have been formed over its long history.*

## 苏　剧

亦称苏州滩簧，为苏州地方戏。本是一种戏曲清唱体曲艺，200多年来，一直流传于江南民间。

### *SUZHOU OPERA*

*It is the local opera of Suzhou, also called "Tanhuang", which has evolved from the local art of singing. It has been most popular among the folks in the southern Yangtze Delta region for over 200 years.*

## 昆　剧

我国现存最古老的戏曲剧种之一，誉称“百戏之祖”。源于元末明初苏州府昆山一带，又称昆曲。

### *KUNQU OPERA*

*One of the oldest theatrical art forms in China and generally regarded as the "origin of classical operas", it had its origin in the area of Kunshan, Suzhou Prefecture, as early as the Yuan Dynasty.*

苏剧《花魁记》 *Suzhou Opera, "the Story of a Beauty".*

昆剧《荆钗记》 *Kunqu Opera, "the Story of Hairpin and Bracelet".*

古戏台 *The traditional stage for theatrical performances.*

山歌 *The book "Mountain Songs".*

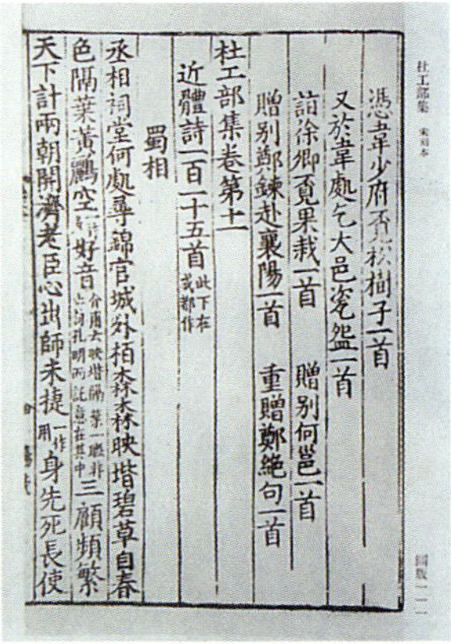
憑韋少府班覓松樹子一首
又於韋處乞大邑瓷盌一首
詣徐卿覓果栽一首　贈別何邕一首
贈別鄭鍊赴襄陽一首　重贈鄭鍊絕句一首
杜工部集卷第十一
近體詩一百一十五首 此下在成都作
蜀相
丞相祠堂何處尋錦官城外柏森森映階碧草自春
色隔葉黃鸝空好音三顧頻繁
天下計兩朝開濟老臣心出師未捷身先死長使

宋刻本 *A specimen of printed book of the Song Dynasty.*

## 苏州刻书

苏州书籍刊刻约起于唐代，明代苏州书坊有四五十家，在全国府县中刻书最多。为文化传播和图书收藏起到了重要作用。

### *BLOCK-PRINTING OF SUZHOU*

*The technique of book printing by carved wood-blocks in Suzhou started in the Tang Dynasty, and in the Ming period, there were as many as forty to fifty printing workshops, which produced more books than any other prefectures and counties of the country, making significant contributions to the spread of culture and the collecting of books.*

## 吴　歌

吴语地区的民间歌谣，俗称“唱山歌”，曾在我国诗歌史上开一代新风。明代有冯梦龙收集整理的吴歌代表作《山歌》、《挂枝儿》。近期发现有长篇叙事吴歌《五姑娘》等，轰动一时。

### *THE WU SONGS*

*The folk songs of the Wu dialect area, also called "the singing of mountain songs", occupy an important chapter in the annals of Chinese poetry. Back in the Ming period, the author Feng Menglong collected and compiled the representative Wu Songs in the books, "Mountain Songs" and "Osmanthus Twigs". The latest finding of Wu Songs in extensive narrative, "the Fifth Sister", made great repercussions in the literary field.*

古籍刻本 *Wood-block printed classical works.*

乱针绣·镇湖苏绣艺术馆

*An embroidery work in crisscross stitch by Zhenhu Embroidery Art Gallery.*

## 苏 绣

我国四大名绣之一。已有两千多年历史，具有精细雅洁的艺术特色。苏州刺绣研究所名作纷出；太湖之滨镇湖镇被文化部命名为“中国刺绣艺术之乡”。镇湖苏绣艺术馆的精品刺绣，传誉国内外。

## *SUZHOU EMBROIDERY*

*Suzhou embroidery is one of the four most famous embroidery schools in China, with a history of over 2,000 years and the special characteristics of being exquisite, delicate, elegant and neat. Suzhou Embroidery Research Institute has produced many masterpieces of embroidery. The town of Zhenhu on the shores of Lake Tai has been declared by the Ministry of Culture as the "home of Chinese embroidery art", and the works from its embroidery art gallery enjoy great reputation both in China and overseas.*

双面绣·苏州刺绣研究所 *Double-sided embroidery work in crisscross stitch by Suzhou Embroidery Research Institute.*

## 桃花坞木刻年画

起源于明，因木刻作坊集中于城内桃花坞一带而得名。清雍、乾年间达全盛时期，对日本“浮世绘”有相当影响。采用一版一色，从现实生活中发掘主题，富有装饰性。作品常出国展出，被誉为“东方古艺之花”。

## *TAOHUAWU WOOD-BLOCK PRINTS OF NEW YEAR PICTURES*

*This art form origninated in the Ming Dynasty, its name referring to the place where most of the studios used to concentrate. Between Yongzheng and Qianlong Reigns of the Qing, the art reached its zenith, giving much influence to the Japanese art of Buse. The highly decorative pictures are printed with a series of blocks, each in one color. The motifs are often taken from daily life. The pictures are often exhibited overseas and hailed as "a flower of the ancient art in the Orient".*

一团和气 *Roly-poly Ball of Harmoney.*

小巷吴歌 · 张晓飞 *"Wu Songs from a Deep Alley" by Zhang Xiaofei.*

姑苏阊门图（清）

*The Changmen Gate of Suzhou (of the Qing Dynasty)*

檀香扇 *Delicate Sandal-Wood Fans.*

澄泥砚 *Chengni Stone Ink-Slabs.*

## 苏扇

苏产扇子总称。苏州制扇约自晋代始，团扇初为宫中之物；竹摺扇扇面向为文人雅士书画领地；檀香扇为苏州首创，芳香馥郁、玲珑精巧。此外香木扇、纸团扇、麦草扇等均为市民、旅游者乐于选用。

### *SUZHOU-STYLE FANS*

*They refer to all kinds of fans made in Suzhou. The craft first appeared in the Jin Dynasty. The silk gauze fans were originally used in royal courts. The bamboo folding fans are used by scholars to display paintings and calligraphy. The sweet-smelling and delicate sandal-wood fans are an invention of Suzhou. Besides, there are perfumed fans, paper fans, and straw fans, popular among tourists and the local folks.*

## 澄泥砚

与端砚、歙砚、洮河砚齐名的中国四大名砚之一。产于藏书镇辖内，已有1700多年历史。其石质细腻，造型奇巧。

### *CHENGNI STONE INK-SLABS*

*Made in the town of Cangshu, the Chengni stone ink-slab is one of the four varieties of Chinese ink-slabs, the others being Duan, She, and Taohe ink-slabs. With a history of over 1,700 years, it features fine grains of stone and novel shapes.*

## 苏　雕

包括木、石、漆、玉、砖、核等雕刻品。苏雕在建筑、旅游、日用、装饰、艺术、文化等各方面均发挥重要作用，在世界艺术之林也具有独特的地位。

### *SUZHOU CARVING*

*An important component in the world of arts, Suzhou carving is done with wood, stone, lacquer, jade, brick, and fruit nuts, etc., found in buildings, tourism facilities, articles for daily use, decoration, art, and culture.*

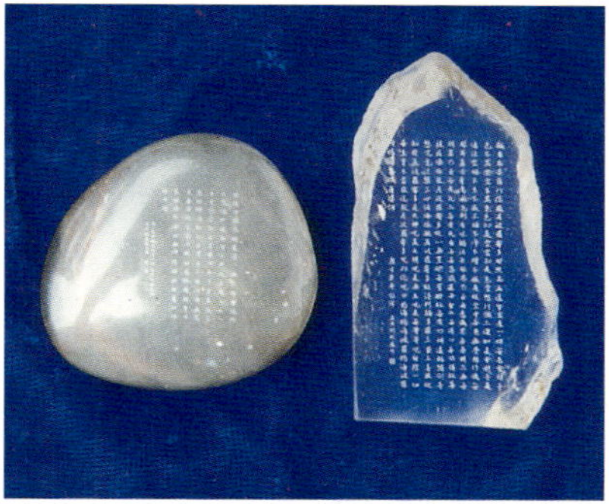

微雕　*Samples of micro-carving.*

石雕茶壶　*Stone-carved tea pots.*

## 缂丝

始创于隋唐，勃兴于宋，有“通经（线）断纬（线）”特点。名师王金山用新技法创作的双面异色异样异技缂丝作品《寿星图》(左上下图)，曾荣获中国工艺美术品百花奖“金杯奖”及珍品称号。

## *HAND-WOVEN SILK TAPESTRY*

*The ancient craft originated in the Sui and Tang Dynasties and thrived in the Song. Its main characteristic is that the warp threads go all the way through, while the weft threads are woven in part to suit the design. The masterpiece "Longevity" was created by the famous artist Wang Jinshan with newly invented techniques, showing different designs and colors on two sides (upper left and upper lower photos).*

吴昌硕书体“寿”字 *The character "longevity" in Wu Changshuo's seal-engraving style.*

仿任伯年画作的“寿星” *The painting "Man of Long Life", by the well-known artist Ren Bainian.*

中国工艺美术大师王金山缂制新作
*The arts and crafts master Wang Jinshan working on his new creation.*

苏裱 *Suzhou Picture-Mounting.*





## 苏　裱

起于宋，盛于明宣德年后，向有“吴裱最善，他处无及”赞评。现吴门画苑裱画高手既可裱新，还可还破旧古画青春。

## *SUZHOU PICTURE-MOUNTING*

*The craft started in the Song and matured by Xuande Reign of the Ming. It is generally regarded as the "best and unrivalled" in China. The craftsmen in Wu Painting Studio can not only mount new pictures, but also repair and restore the ancient and worn-out pictures.*

## 苏　乐

苏州民族乐器的历史最早可追溯到春秋时期。明代时昆曲的兴起又促进了苏州乐器的发展。苏锣、苏鼓、二胡、琵琶等在国内素负盛名。

## *SUZHOU MUSICAL INSTRUMENTS*

*The making of musical instruments in Suzhou can be traced to the Spring and Autumn Period, but it is most flourishing during the Ming period when Kunqu Opera became popular. Gongs, drums, 2-stringed fiddles, and 4-stinged lutes from Suzhou are much sought after in China.*

苏乐 *Suzhou Musical Instruments.*

## 苏　灯

苏州著名手工艺品，早在南宋时已闻名全国。有造型优美、灯饰华丽、花样出奇的特点。如今，在继承传统技艺基础上，运用新技术、新工艺，苏灯更显光彩、生动。

## *SUZHOU LANTERNS*

*A traditional handicraft which first made its name in the Song period, Suzhou-style lanterns are beautifully shaped, elaborately decorated, and varied in designs. Today, new techniques are integrated with the tradition to add luster and vividness to the art.*

鸡丝馄饨 · 绿杨馄饨店
*Shredded chicken dumplings from Luyang Restaurant.*

## 苏式糕团 SUZHOU-STYLE PASTRY

花式糕团 · 黄天源 *Assorted cakes.*

萝卜丝团 · 黄天源 *Shredded radish cakes.*

八宝饭 · 黄天源 *8-jewels rice pudding from Huangtianyuan Restaurant.*

南瓜猪油糕 · 黄天源 *Pumpkin and pig-fat rice cakes.*

枣泥拉糕 · 新聚丰 *Date rice-cakes from Xinjufeng Restaurant.*

南塘鸡头 · 得月楼 *Nantang Gorgon fruit soup from Deyuelou Restaurant.*

生煎馒头 · 三德利食府 *Fried minced pies from Sandeli Restaurant.*

百合绿豆汤 · 得月楼 *Sweetmeat of lili and green beans.*

三色圆子 · 得月楼 *Tri-color dumplings from Deyuelou Restaurant.*

五彩荷花酥 · 金都饭店 *5-color lotus-shaped fried cakes.*

## 苏式菜肴 SUZHOU CUISINE

松鼠鳜鱼 · 松鹤楼 *Squirrel-shaped mandarin fish*

西施玩月 · 得月楼 *Quail eggs soup from Deyuelou Restaurant.*

鲃肺汤 · 石家饭店 *River fish-lung soup from Shijia Restaurant.*

鳝筒虎皮蛋 · 新聚丰 *River eel with fried eggs from Xinjufeng Restaurant.*

金都八宝盒 · 金都饭店 *Jindu 8-Jewel pastry from Jindu Restaurant.*

秘制酱鸭 · 陆稿荐 *Sweet-sauced Duck from Lugaojian Deli.*

卤汁豆腐干 · 津津 *Sweetened bean-curd from Jinjin Food Store.*

黄埭西瓜子 · 天福 *Huangdai Melon seeds from Tianfu Factory.*

虾子鲞鱼 · 叶受和 *Salt Yangtze Shad flavored with shrimp eggs.*

粽子糖 · 采芝斋 *Caltrop-shaped candy from Caizhizhai Confectionery.*

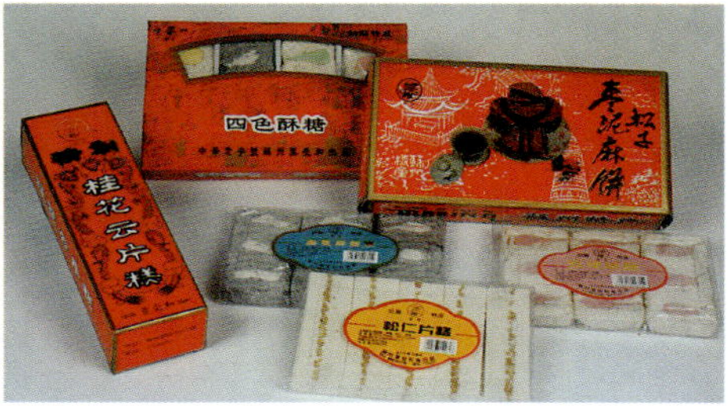


糕点 · 叶受和 *Cakes from Yeshouhe Confectionery.*

酥糖 · 采芝斋 *Sesame sweets from Caizhizhai Confectionery.*

苏式糖果 · 叶受和 *Suzhou-style sweets from Yeshohe .*

枣泥麻饼 · 采芝斋 *Sesame cakes with jujube jam .*

茶园 *A tea plantation.*

阳澄湖大闸蟹 *Giant freshwater crabs from Yangcheng Lake.*

碧螺春茶 *The green tea "Bilouchun".*

太湖白虾 *White-skinned shrimps from Lake Tai.*

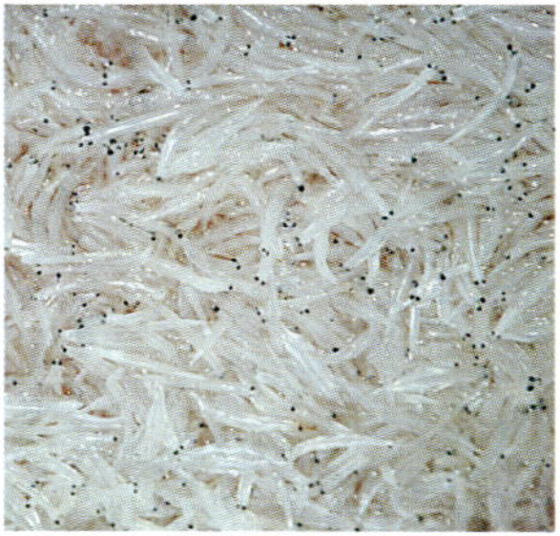

太湖银鱼 *Silver fish from Lake Tai.*

洞庭桔 *Tangerines from Dongting Hills.*

洞庭西山石榴 *Pomegranates from West Dongting Hill.*

洞庭西山枇杷 *Loquats from West Dongting Hill.*

水红菱 *Red water caltrops.*

洞庭西山白果 *Gingko nuts from West Dongting Hill.*

洞庭西山板栗 *Chestnuts from West Dongting Hill.*

洞庭东山杨梅 *Bay-berries from East Dongting Hill.*

中央公园
*The Central Park*

中新合作纪念雕塑

*Commemorative sculpture for China-Singapore co-operation.*

## 苏州工业园区

位于古城东侧，是中国和新加坡两国政府的合作项目。发展目标是建设一个以高新技术为先导、现代工业为主体，第三产业和社会公益事业相配套的国际化现代化工业园区。已有一大批世界著名跨国公司入驻开业。

## *SUZHOU INDUSTRIAL PARK*

*Situated on the eastern flank of the ancient city, Suzhou Industrial Park is development project through cooperation between the governments of China and Singapore, aimed to build up a modern international industrial park focused on new and hi-tech with all-round coordinated development of service industries and social amenities. At present, a great number of well-known multi-national companies have invested and started operation in the industrial park.*

园区管委会
*The building of Suzhou Industrial Park Administrative Committee.*

园区街景 *A street scene in the industrial park.*

园区新貌
*The fresh look of the industrial park.*

新区雄姿
The grand view of Suzhou New District.

## 苏州新区

位于古城西侧，为国家级高新科技产业开发区。区内已形成电子信息、生物医药、光机电一体化、新材料、环保节能净化技术等支柱产业。已有住友、飞利浦、爱普生等世界级企业进驻。

## *SUZHOU NEW DISTRICT*

*Situated on the west of the ancient city proper, Suzhou New District is a national new and hi-tech industrial development zone. Its major industries are IT, bio-medicine, integrated optical and electronic machinery, new materials, and energy-saving purification equipment for environmental protection. A number of world-famous companies like Philips, Sumitomo, and Epson have settled down in the District.*

公园一景 *A scene in the park.*

中心雕塑 *The central sculpture.*

## 飞利浦消费电子公司

荷兰飞利浦公司与苏州电视机厂合资建立的彩电生产企业。建成以来，运用先进管理方法和高新技术开发出的新品不断涌现，销售收入名列苏州市企业之首。

## *PHILIPS HOUSEHOLD ELECTRONIC COMPANY*

*It is a joint venture established by Philips and Suzhou TV Factory for the manufacturing of color TV sets. Ever since its founding, the company has developed many new products on the basis of advanced management and the development of new and high technology, and consequently its sales revenue has ranked the very top in Suzhou.*

## 宁沪高速公路阳澄湖服务区

位于阳澄湖畔，东距上海60公里，西距苏州12公里。服务区设餐厅、客房、大小会议室、超市、加油站等场所，为过往旅客提供餐饮、住宿、购物等服务。服务区水产市场为江苏省“文明市场”，每年可提供“菊黄”牌阳澄湖大闸蟹500吨供顾客选购。

### *YANGCHENG LAKE SERVICE AREA OF NANJING-SHANGHAI EXPRESSWAY*

*60 kilometers west of Shanghai and 12 kilometers east of Suzhou, the service area provide travelers with facilities of restaurants, guestrooms, various sizes of meeting rooms, supermarket, and gas station. Besides, there is a market of aquatic products, which has been awarded the title of "civilized market", where 500 tons of the "Yellow Chrysanthemum" brand giant freshwater crabs from Yangcheng Lake are offered annually for customers' choice.*

沪宁高速公路 *Shanghai-Nanjing Expressway.*

宁沪高速公路阳澄湖服务区 *Yangcheng Lake Service Area of NANJING-SHANGHAI Expressway.*

得月楼
*Deyuelou Restaurant.*

## 得月楼

明代嘉靖年间开设在山塘街野芳浜口，现坐落在市中心太监弄，以苏帮特色菜见长。有蟹黄扒翅、碧螺虾仁、奶汤鲫鱼、得月童鸡等名菜佳肴。

### *DEYUELOU RESTAURANT*

*This restaurant of Suzhou cuisine was founded at Yefangbang, Shantang Street during Jia Jing Reign of the Ming. Now it is relocated on Taijian Lane in the downtown shopping center. Its famous dishes are crabmeat with shark's fin, shelled shrimps with green tea, Silver carp in white soup, and Deyue chicken, etc.*

## 叶受和

坐落于观前街。开创于清光绪十一年（1885年），以自产特色糕点、糖果、炒货等见长，著名产品八珍糕、肉松、野味、虾子鲞鱼等脍炙人口。

### *YESHOUHE CONFECTIONERY*

*Located on Guanqian Street and founded in the 11th year of Guangxu Reign of the Qing, the confectionery is reputed for its own products of sweets, cakes, and fried nuts. Among the famous are 8-jewel puddings, Fluffy meat, wild poultry, and shrimp-egg flavored cuttlefish, etc.*

采芝斋 *Caizhizhai Confectionery.*

叶受和 *Yeshouhe Confectionery.*

## 采芝斋

位于观前街。始创于清同治九年（1870年），独创的粽子糖最为盛名，曾被慈禧太后命为“贡糖”。现生产的苏式糖果品种更多。苏式蜜饯、炒货、糕点等也是其拿手精品。

### *CAIZHIZHAI CONFECTIONERY*

*Founded on Guanqian Street in the 9th year of Tong Chi Reign of the Qing, the confectionery is most famous for its caltrop-shaped candies, which Empress Dowager named "imperial tribute". The range of sweets have now greatly widened. Its traditional products also include Suzhou-style preserved fruits, fried nuts, and pastry, etc.*

苏州丝绸瑞富祥专卖店 *Ruifuxiang Suzhou Silk Special Store.*

坦桑尼亚总统夫人访瑞富祥

*A visit to the store by the wife of Tanzanian President.*

## 瑞富祥

苏州丝绸瑞富祥专卖店位于石路南端，是瑞富祥纺织品有限公司的下属商店。该店实行衣料服饰零卖、设计、制作一条龙服务，提供自制的“绣娘”品牌丝绸制品与各种名牌丝绸面料。为苏州市、金阊区“巾帼文明示范岗”。

### *RUIFUXIANG SILK STORE*

*On the southern section of Shilu Road, it is a special retail store of local silk fabrics affiliated to Ruifuxiang Textile Co., Ltd., offering complete services in retail, design, and custom-making of garment and ornament. It sells the "Embroidery Girl" brand silks produced by its own company as well as other famous brands of yardage.*

## 人民商场

地处观前商业中心，营业面积达2.5万平方米，为综合性大型商场，经营名优商品8万余种。设有多种服务部门，具备集购物、休闲、美食、娱乐于一体的整体功能优势。

*THE PEOPLE'S EMPORIUM*

*Located by Guanqian Street in the shopping center, this large-scale comprehensive department store has a total floor space of 25,000 square meters for business. Apart from the over 80,000 items of quality goods, there are multi-purpose facilities for leisure, recreation, food and beverage.*

人民商场 *The People's Emporium.*

工业品商场、购物中心
*The Industrial Goods Store and Shopping Center.*

## 工业品商场、购物中心

坐落在察院场，营业面积2万平方米，苏州大型商场之一。经营商品30多个大类，达几万种。开创有汽车、文物、字画拍卖、对外贸易等多种经销领域。

*THE INDUSTRIAL GOODS STORE AND SHOPPING CENTER*

*Located at Chayuanchang crossroad, it is one the largest department stores in Suzhou, with a business area of 20,000 square meters and 30 categories of goods in thousands of varieties. It has recently initialed the auction of vehicles, antiques, paintings and calligraphy as well as export business.*

酒店夜景 *The night view of the hotel.*

大堂 *A hall.*

包厢 *A private dining room.*

## 君怡大酒店

位于石路商贸中心，主楼13层，为中外合作经营大酒店与涉外旅游饭店。酒店按三星级标准设置。酒店餐饮独树一帜，特色菜肴有松鼠鳜鱼、避风塘肉蟹、樱桃汁肉等。

## *JUNYI HOTEL*

*Located in the Shilu commercial area, the 13-story hotel is a 3-star international tourist hotel managed through Sino-foreign cooperation, specially known for its food and beverage service, such as the squirrel-shaped mandarin fish, Bifengtang sea crab, and cherry-flavored meat, etc.*

★★★★★

### 新苏国际大酒店

苏州市第一家五星级大酒店。位于工业园区金鸡湖畔，西洋别墅式与古典园林式建筑有机地建造在一起，令人耳目一新。细意浓情的服务，高档完善的设施，是政要会晤、商务考察、会议度假的最佳场所。

*NEW SUZHOU INTERNATIONAL HOTEL*

*The first 5-star hotel built in Suzhou, it is located by Jinji Lake in a combined style of Western villa and classical Chinese Garden architecture. Its superb quality service makes it an ideal place for official receptions, business tours, conferences, and vacations.*

酒店一隅 *A part of the hotel.*

总统楼 *The presidential suite.*

酒店远眺 *The distant view of the hotel.*

## 苏州乐园

地处新区狮子山麓，占地94万平方米，首期工程水上世界建成以来，已成为华东地区夏季旅游热点。二期工程欢乐世界以“东方迪斯尼”为主题，引进时空飞船、太空历险和三角翼、迷的洋馆等一大批高科技游乐设施。被誉为“中国新生代主题乐园的点睛之作”。

## *SUZHOU AMUSEMENT LAND*

*Built at the foot of Lion Hill in Suzhou New District with an area of 940,000 square meters, the amusement park has become a popular tourist spot in East China since the completion of its Phase 1. The Phase 2 project, the Joyful World, takes "Disney of the East" as its theme and launched hi-tech entertainment facilities such as the time-and-space ship, the space adventure, the triangle wings, and the Midi-hall, etc. The amusement park is praised as "a masterpiece of theme park of a new generation in China".*

乐园美景 *A grand view of the Amusement Land.*

豪华波浪 *Fashion in waves.*

童话王国 *The kingdom of fairy tales.*

中兴高尔夫球场 *Zhongxing Golf Course.*

星海游泳馆 *Xinghai Swimming Complex.*

## 旅游服务单位：
## Tourism Services:

| 单　　位 Name | TEL | 单　　位 Name | TEL |
| --- | --- | --- | --- |
| 君怡大酒店　Junyi Hotel | 5325198 | 人民商场　The People's Emporium | 5221252 |
| 新苏国际大酒店　New Suzhou International Hotel | 7616688 | 工业品商场、购物中心　Industrial Goods Store & Shopping Center | 7275324 |
| 得月楼菜馆　Deyuelou Restaurant | 5233027 | 苏州丝绸瑞富祥专卖店　Ruifuxiang Suzhou Silk Special Store | 5561998 |
| 新聚丰菜馆　Xinjufeng Restaurant | 5219940 | 镇湖刺绣厂　Zhenhu Embroidery Factory | 6911241 |
| 松鹤楼菜馆　Songhelou Restaurant | 7277006 | 西山供销社（土特产专卖）West Hill Supply & Marketing Cooperative (for Local Produce) | 6271519 |
| 石家饭店　Shijia Restaurant | 5212987 | 吴都茶叶有限公司　Wudu Tea Co., Ltd. | 8258419 |
| 绿杨馄饨店　Luyang Dumpling Restaurant | 7284732 | 宁沪高速公路阳澄湖服务区 Yangcheng Lake Service Area Nanjing-Shanghai Expressway | 5079657 |
| 黄天源糕团店　Huangtianyuan Pastry Store | 7277033 | 苏州乐园　Suzhou Amusement Land | 8252036 |
| 采芝斋糖果店　Caizhizhai Confectionery | 7276222 | 第一人民医院　No. 1 People's Hospital | 5223637 |
| 叶受和糖果店　Yeshouhe Confectionery | 7709603 | 旅游投诉　Tourist Complaints | 5223377 |

## 旅游交通指南：
## Tourist Transport Directory:

| 线路 Bus Number | 停靠站 Stops |
| --- | --- |
| 游1东线 | 虎丘→西园→留园→石路→艺圃→环秀山庄→观前街→玄妙观→狮子林→拙政园→北寺塔→火车站 |
| 游2线 | 火车站→北寺塔→拙政园→狮子林→观前街→双塔→第一人民医院→网师园→沧浪亭→盘门景区 |
| 游3线 | 火车站→山塘街→西园→寒山寺→苏州乐园→水上乐园 |
| 游4线 | 火车站→北寺塔→观前街→怡园→沧浪亭→唐寅墓→横塘→木渎→灵岩山→天平山 |
| 吴越春秋线 | 火车站→北寺塔→观前街→饮马桥→胥门→附二医院→横塘→石湖→吴越春秋 |
| 周庄、角直线 | 火车站→观前街（东）→角直→锦溪→周庄 |
| 同里线 | 火车站→观前街（东）→汽车南站→同里 |
| 西山线 | 火车站→观前街（东）→十梓街→狮山大桥→木渎→胥口→太湖大桥→林屋洞→石公山 |
| 东山线（中巴） | 吴县汽车站→木渎→东山 |
| 光福线（中巴） | 吴县汽车站→木渎→藏书→光福 |

太湖风景名胜区(苏州)导游图
A Tourist Map of Lake Tai Historical and Scenic Areas (Suzhou)
N
虞山景区
Yushan Hill Scenic Area
常熟市
翁同和墓
黄公望墓
兴福寺
言子庙
仲雍墓
尚湖
昆承湖
无锡市
Wuxi City
沪宁高速
312国道
洛社
石塘湾
西漳
张泾
东湖
查桥
前桥
羊尖
练塘镇
张桥
沙家浜
唐市
荡口
辛庄
北桥
湘城
东降
新安
硕放
渭塘
阳澄湖
巴城镇
马山区
南泉
望亭
东桥
黄埭
昆山
Kunshan
通安
陆慕
正仪
中国刺绣艺术之乡
镇湖
万佛石塔
光福景区
Guangfu Scenic Area
香雪海
光福
司徒庙
天池山
华山
枫桥
天平山
寒山寺
苏州市
斜塘
胜浦
藏书
灵岩山
穹窿山
木渎景区
Mudu Scenic Area
木渎
上方山
石湖
郭巷
车坊
甪直
保圣寺
甪直景区
Luzhi Scenic Area
澄湖
中国书画之乡
太湖国家旅游度假区
石湖景区
Stone Lake Scenic Area
越溪
周里景区
Tongli Scenic Area
同里
浦庄
横泾
吴江市
Wujiang City
退思园
太湖大桥
禹王庙
林屋洞
罗汉寺
西山
西山景区
West Hill Scenic Area
石公山
渡村
启园
东山
春在楼
陆巷
紫金庵
明善堂
东山景区
East Hill Scenic Area
东太湖
周庄
Zhouzhuang Township
金家坝
莘塔
八坼
北厍
横扇
318国道
庙港
梅堰
黎里
平望
太湖